A long time ago,
As a little girl,
I dreamed of traveling
All over the world,
And often I think
About the most
Driving everyone
Crazy fast!

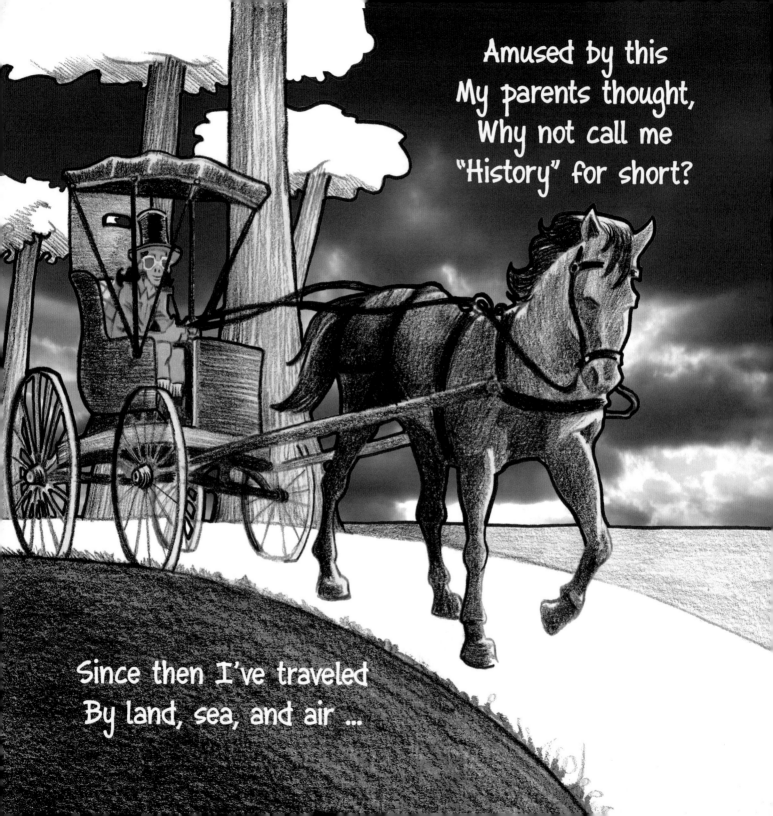

Little Miss HISTORY Travels to
FORD'S THEATER

Published in
The UNITED STATES of AMERICA
eugenus® STUDIOS, Publisher
P.O. BOX 112
CRARYVILLE, NY 12521
E-Mail: Barbara@LittleMissHistory.com
WebSite: www.LittleMissHISTORY.com

ISBN-13: 978-0-9885030-4-5
ISBN-10: 0988503042

Dedicated to ...

... all my grandchildren,
those already here:

Ava, Theresa, Dougie, Sammie,
Emma, Hannah, Jamie,

and those to come ...

BARBARA ANN MOJICA'S

Little Miss HISTORY®

Travels to

FORD'S THEATER

Illustrations by VICTOR RAMON MOJICA

Here we are at Ford's Theater, in Washington D.C., the Capital of the United States of America.

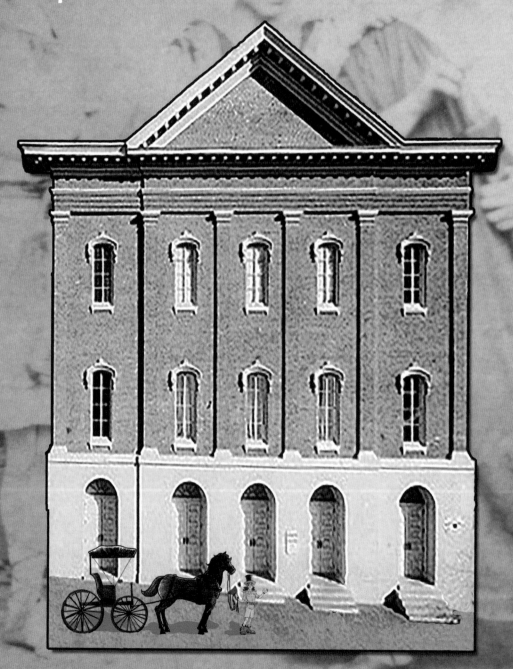

It started out as a meeting house for the First Baptist Church of Washington in 1833 with Obadiah Bruen Brown as its pastor.

In 1861 John T. Ford renovated it into a theater called Ford's Athenaeum.

An athenaeum is a place where learning is encouraged. Ford's Athenaeum burned to the ground one year later.

Ford rebuilt it in 1863 to seat 2400 people calling the theater a "magnificent thespian temple." The word "thespian" means an actor or a drama in a theater.

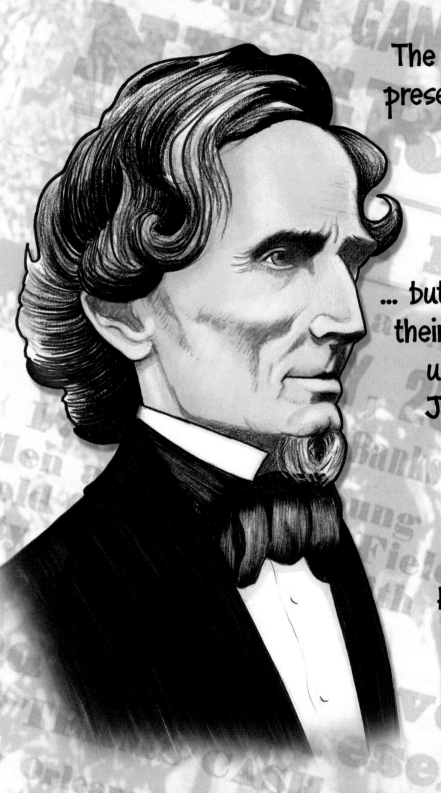

The North fought to preserve the Union ...

... but the South set up their own government under President Jefferson Davis.

They fought to keep their slave based economy.

The war lasted
four horrible years!
On April 9th, 1865,
it ended.

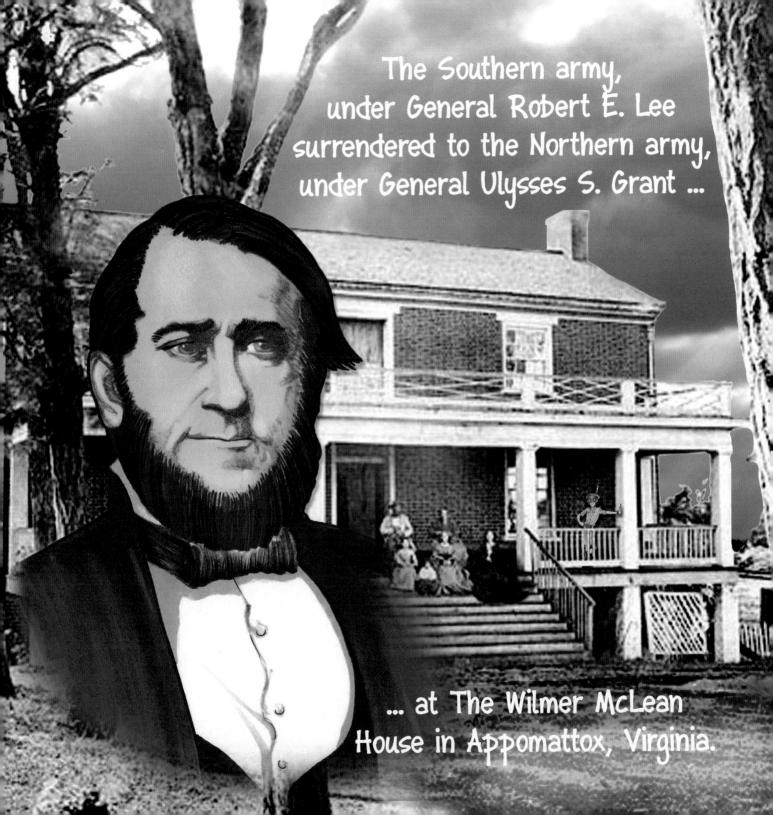

The Southern army,
under General Robert E. Lee
surrendered to the Northern army,
under General Ulysses S. Grant ...

... at The Wilmer McLean
House in Appomattox, Virginia.

Five days later, President Abraham Lincoln and his wife Mary attended the stage play *Our American Cousin* at Ford's Theater.

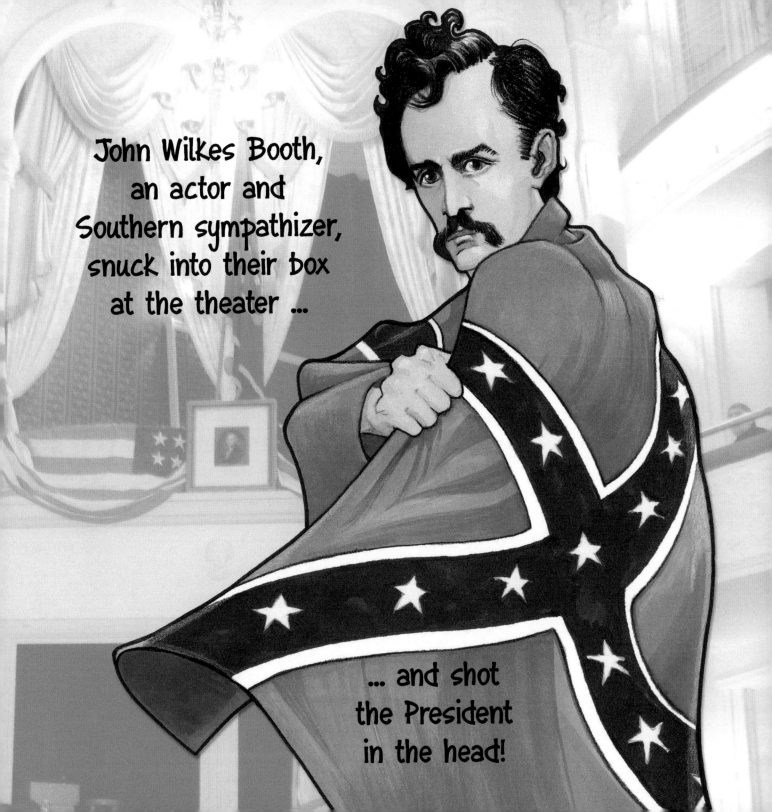

Leaping onto
the stage,
Booth cried out in Latin,
"Sic semper tyrannis!"
(Thus always to tyrants)
Some thought they
heard him say,
"The South is avenged!"

Booth then escaped on horseback from the theater's back alley.

The mortally wounded Abraham Lincoln was carried to the Petersen House just across the street from Ford's Theater.

A Canadian-born black doctor named Anderson Ruffin Abbott sadly watched as the man who had freed the slaves in America lay dying.

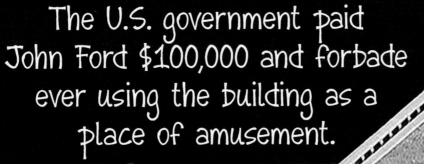

The U.S. government paid John Ford $100,000 and forbade ever using the building as a place of amusement.

The War Department used the building for many years.

By 1918 American lawmakers had begun to think about restoring it. After fifty years, it reopened as a theater.

The U.S. government decided to make both Ford's Theater and the Petersen House a National Historic Site in 1932.

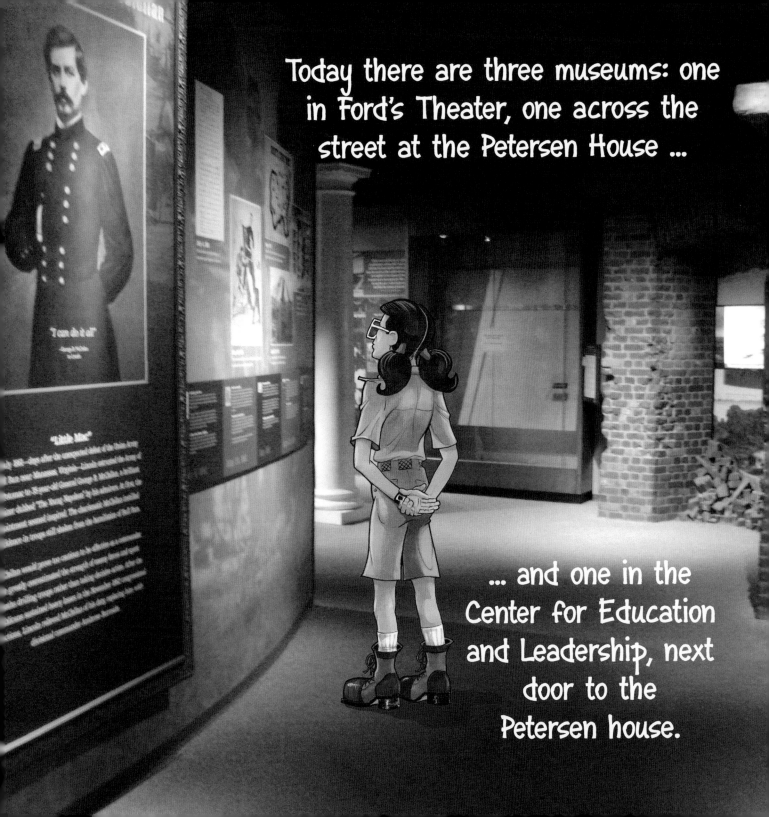

Today there are three museums: one in Ford's Theater, one across the street at the Petersen House ...

... and one in the Center for Education and Leadership, next door to the Petersen house.

There is so much to see such as the Derringer pistol that Booth used to shoot Lincoln ...

... the boot he wore in his escape from Ford's Theater ...

... a shawl that Lincoln wore ...

Between visits to her husband's bedside, Mary Lincoln waited in this parlor with her son Robert and friends of the Lincoln family.

... and the bed where Lincoln passed away.

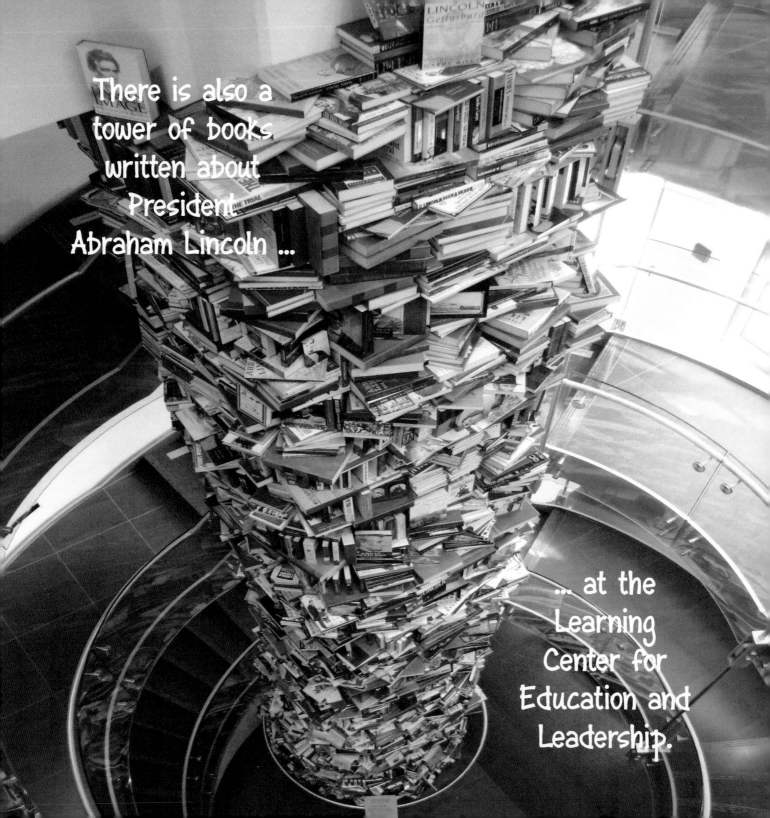

There is also a tower of books written about President Abraham Lincoln ...

... at the Learning Center for Education and Leadership.

Next Stop ...

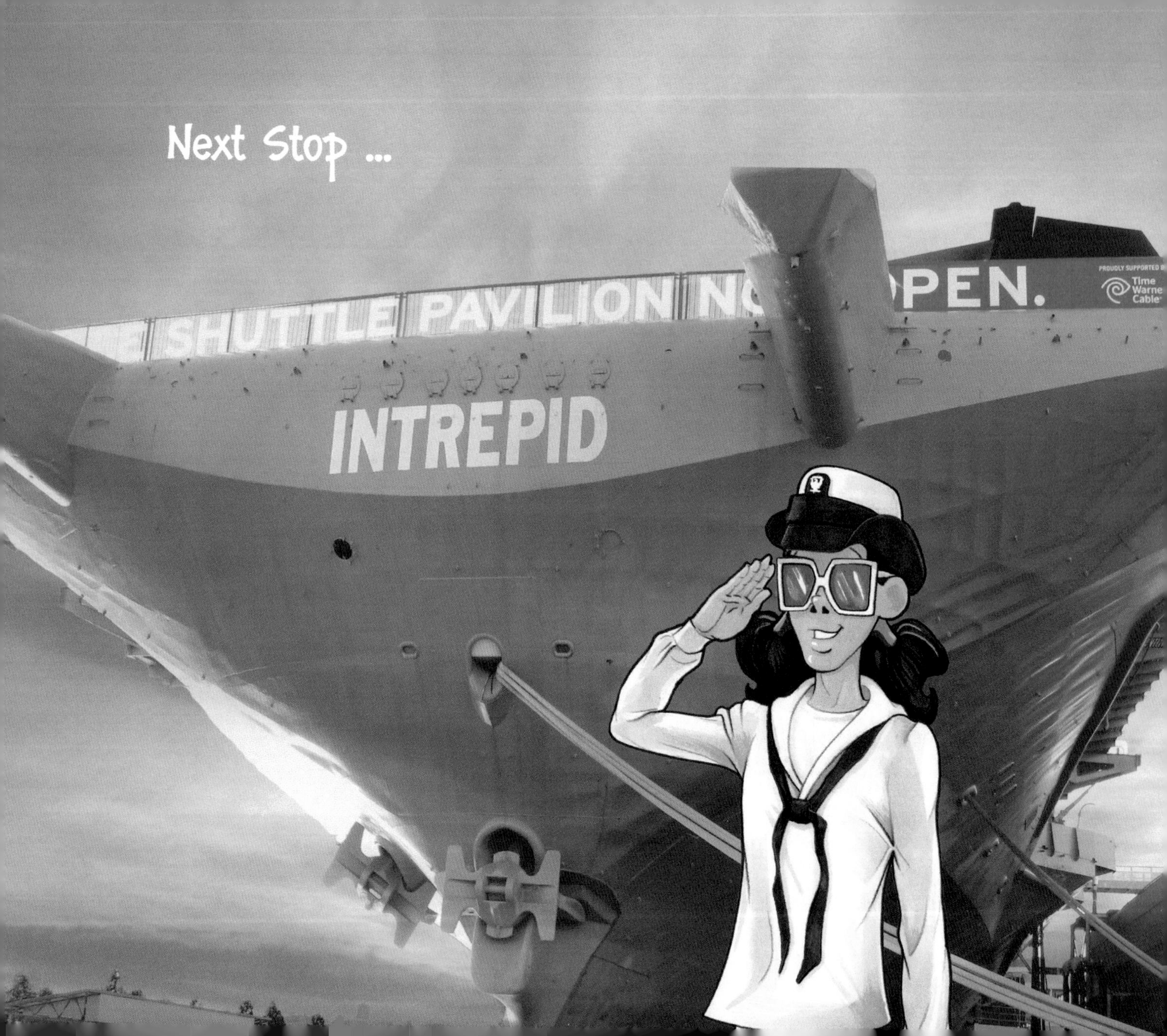